Maxed Out

Maxed Out

Daphne Greer

orca currents

ORCA BOOK PUBLISHERS

Library and Archives Canada Cataloguing in Publication

Greer, Daphne
Maxed out / Daphne Greer.
(Orca currents)

Issued also in electronic formats.
ISBN 978-1-55469-981-0 (pbk.).--ISBN 978-1-55469-982-7 (bound)

I. Title. II. Series: Orca currents.
PS8613.R4452M39 2012   JC813'.6   C2011-907574-1

First published in the United States, 2012
Library of Congress Control Number: 2011942585

Summary: Twelve-year-old Max struggles to manage a grieving mother,
a special-needs brother and a desire to play hockey.

MIX
Paper from
responsible sources
FSC® C016245

*Orca Book Publishers is dedicated to preserving the environment and has printed
this book on paper certified by the Forest Stewardship Council®.*

Orca Book Publishers gratefully acknowledges the support for its
publishing programs provided by the following agencies: the Government
of Canada through the Canada Book Fund and the Canada Council for the Arts,
and the Province of British Columbia through the BC Arts Council
and the Book Publishing Tax Credit.

Cover photography by Dreamstime.com
Author photo by Sharon Alexander

ORCA BOOK PUBLISHERS
PO Box 5626, Stn. B
Victoria, BC Canada
V8R 6S4

ORCA BOOK PUBLISHERS
PO Box 468
Custer, WA USA
98240-0468

www.orcabook.com
Printed and bound in Canada.

15 14 13 12 • 4 3 2 1

To Michael Rodriguez, who brings sunshine and light to everyone he meets.

Chapter One

The sound of the back door banging against the side of the house pounds in my ears. Maybe I am only hearing my heart beating in my chest as I pick up my pace. I trudge up the driveway with my sleeping bag hanging over my shoulder. I kick snow away from the step.

"Mom!" I yell. "I'm home."

The house is quiet. I dump my backpack on the floor and flick my boots off. The cold air has made a home in the kitchen. I can see my breath. Dishes are piled in the sink, and breakfast stuff is still all over the counter. When I walk down the hall, I glance into the living room. It looks like time has stopped. Mom doesn't go in there much anymore. It used to be her favorite place.

At the bottom of the stairs, I stop to listen. I'm relieved when I hear Duncan talking to himself in his room. It sounds like he is acting out all the characters in a movie. When I reach the landing, I notice Mom's bedroom door is closed.

I take a deep breath and knock. "Mom?"

I can hear her stirring, so I open the door. She is lying in bed with heaps of blankets piled all over her. "Oh, Max. You're home. I didn't hear you come in." She tries to sit up, but she only gets as far as propping herself onto her elbows before she flops back down. She pulls the blankets up to her neck. "It's freezing in here. Can you check the heat?" She yawns and then says, "What time is it?"

"I don't know. Probably close to four. The bus was a little late."

"Did you say *four*? That can't be right! I only laid down for a few minutes. Oh, I can't believe it!" She looks like she's about to cry. "I have to work tonight, and I feel like a truck hit me."

"I'll go check the heat," I say. I don't bother telling her that the back door was wide open or that I had a great time at the school winter-survival trip at Big Cove Camp. I don't tell her about making banana boats around the campfire, like we used to do with Dad, or how we stayed up late telling ghost stories. No one wanted to go home— especially me.

The next morning I'm in a rush. I'm still not used to having to do everything by myself.

"Duncan!" I yell up the stairs. "Turn off the TV. We're going to be late!" I wait at the the bottom of the stairs for a few more minutes. Duncan is deep into one of his movies. I shake my head and walk back toward the kitchen. The sun floods in through the window, making it really warm.

Duncan eventually shuffles into the kitchen with his Spider-Man T-shirt on backward and his hair sticking up. "I'm not Duncan. I'm Spider-Man!"

"No one will know you're Spider-Man with your shirt on *that* way," I say.

Duncan stands perfectly still while I stand on my tiptoes to turn his shirt around. "Where is Mom?" he asks.

I glance at the clock. "She's at work," I say.

"I don't like her work," he says.

"Neither do I. Come on, we've got to hurry." I pour cereal into his bowl. Usually I let him do it, but we're already late. I don't have time for him to pour it, spill it and then pick up each piece of cereal.

"Do you wanna race?" I ask.

"I'm not racing," he grumbles.

I inhale my cereal and then start running around grabbing our stuff. When I open the back door, the cold air hits me smack in the face. "Man, that's freezing. You're going to need a hat today, Duncan."

"I don't want one," he mumbles.

"I hear ya. But remember your ears hurt when it's really cold. Besides, Spider-Man wouldn't be caught dead going out without his hat."

Duncan shovels another mouthful of his cereal into his mouth. I can tell he is thinking about what I said. "I want my hat," he says.

"I figured you would." I throw it to him. He lifts his hand at the right moment and catches it, even though he's not looking at me. Duncan avoids eye contact at any cost. He places his hat on his head and takes two more bites of cereal. Then he pushes his bowl away and says, "I'm done."

Outside, the cold air stings my nose. I pull the collar of my coat up as far as it will go.

Our next-door neighbor, Mr. Cooper, is bent down picking up his newspaper. He's usually the only person we see on our street in the morning. He never has his winter coat on, and he wears pants that are way too big for him. Sometimes I wonder if he used to be really big and then lost a bunch of weight but forgot to buy proper clothes afterward. He's nice to Duncan and me. "Hi, Max. Hi, Duncan. It's a little nippy today, eh?"

"I'm Spider-Man," Duncan says.

I smile at Mr. Cooper. He is used to Duncan.

"Sorry, Spider-Man," Mr. Cooper says. "One of these days I'll get it right."

"You're going to confuse him," I say to Duncan once we're out of earshot. "Yesterday you were Batman, and the day before you were Darth Vader!"

"I saw the crack in his bum," Duncan says.

"Well, at least you didn't say that to him." I glance back, but Mr. Cooper is already inside his house.

At the end of the road, we slip into the woods and walk along the path. The snow is deep, but someone has made a trail we can follow. The sun pokes through the tall trees. When we reach the pond, I walk over to the edge and step onto the ice. I get swallowed up in a memory.

There was a full moon, and Dad and I had sneaked out to skate on the pond.

We played some hockey, and then I challenged him to a race. I stare at the ice, remembering Dad. In my mind I hear the scrape of the skates as we darted across the pond and the sound of his belly laugh when we reached the other side. Our race ended in a tie. I know he could have beat me, but that was Dad.

The school bell rings in the distance, pulling me back into the present. Duncan and I turn away from the pond and everything that used to matter.

When we get to Duncan's classroom, I open the door as Lilly slips out. She has the attendance book in her hands. "Oh, you made it just in time." She turns around. "Miss d'Entremont, Duncan is here."

"I'm Spider-Man," he reminds her.

"Oh, sorry, Spider-Man. Hi, Max." Lilly smiles at me with a mouthful of hot pink braces.

"Hey—can't talk," I say. "I'm late again."

Lilly's smile fades, or maybe I'm imagining things. I hurry to class. I can't get another late slip. That would mean a call home.

I run the rest of the way, duck into my classroom and slump down in my chair. Ian is laughing with some kids in the back of the class. No one seems to have a care in the world.

Chapter Two

I can hear them. It's like I'm right there.

I probably know who just scored. The sound of laughter echoes through the woods. When Duncan and I round the bend in the path, Ian is sliding belly-up on the ice. He skids smack into the goalie, puck and all.

"And he scores!" Ian yells.

"Nice one!" I shout in his direction.

"Oweee, nice one," Duncan mimics in a low voice.

Ian stands up and brushes the snow off his pants. "Hey! Can you play today?" he hollers.

"No," I yell back. "Mom's got a long shift." This is my standard answer now. Even when she isn't at work, I still have to say that.

It kills me. I want to skate with Ian and the guys like I used to.

Ian skates over to the side of the pond. "That's a drag!"

"Tell me about it," I say.

Duncan starts walking in circles with his fist in his mouth. I roll my eyes at Ian and then say to Duncan, "We're going in a second! Do you really have to *do* that?"

Duncan ignores me.

"Can't you work something out?" Ian whispers. "He could hang out here while we skate."

"I wish," I say. "Look at him."

Duncan is now crouched down, eating snow.

"Well, you gotta play next Friday, Max," says Ian. "We've got a game with the Red Eagles. I don't want to play against Cody without you."

"I'll see what I can do."

Ian glances back at the guys on the ice. "Okay, I better go. See ya..." He zooms across the pond and steals the puck.

I smile to myself as I pretend I'm on the ice. Then I turn toward Duncan.

"Would you stop eating the snow. For all you know, a dog could have peed on it."

Duncan puts his face closer to the snow. "Nope, no dog pee." He eats another handful.

"I give up. Come on, let's go home." With one last look back at the pond, I lead the way along the path. The sounds of the skates scratching the ice and the shouts from the guys repeat in my head long after we're out of earshot.

"I'm hungry," Duncan says.

"You should have eaten more snow," I say underneath my breath.

The smell of smoke from Mr. Cooper's fireplace means we're almost home. It signals food to Duncan and reminds me of the days when Mom was in the kitchen watching soaps on TV while she made us a snack.

All that changed when Dad died. Dads aren't supposed to die before their kids are grown up. But mine did.

Some days it feels like my mom did too.

As I open the door, Mouse gets up from his sunny spot in the kitchen. He stretches and walks over to us. He rubs up against Duncan's legs and then mine.

"Hi, Mouse," Duncan says. He reaches down to pat him. Mouse purrs loudly. Duncan hangs his coat on his hook and places his boots so that the toes touch the wall. He then straightens all the shoes into a perfect straight line.

I dump my coat on the chair and throw my hat like a Frisbee. "Yes!" I say when it lands on the hook. Usually it takes me a couple of tries.

"I'm hungry," Duncan says.

I'm staring into the fridge, trying to figure out how I can play hockey. I hear Duncan, but I'm too busy thinking to answer.

"I'm *hungry*!" Duncan wails.

The sound of something landing on the floor with a thud startles me. I slam the fridge door. Duncan is on his hands and knees like he is praying.

Sighing, I squat down beside him. "Do you really have to *do* that?"

He doesn't answer. He keeps talking about how his superpowers aren't working because he's so hungry.

"Duncan!" I say in a louder voice.

"Yeah?" he finally says.

"I'll get you something to eat, *okay*?"

"Okay." Duncan sits up and looks at me with his big brown eyes. "I'm hungry," he whimpers.

"I know you are." I hold out my hand and help him stand up. "Let me guess. Macaroni and cheese?"

Duncan smiles.

"At least you're predictable."

"I'm not predictable! I'm, I'm Batman. And, and, you're Robin," he says in a low voice.

"Whatever you say."

On Saturday morning the usual crowd is coming in and out of Bucky Dwayne's All-In-One Store. "Duncan, hurry up!" Three people slip through the door before he catches up to me.

Inside, I pull out the list Mom gave me before she crawled back into bed.

I hate it when she works the night shift, because Duncan has to go everywhere with me so she can sleep. Saturday is the worst day to come to Bucky Dwayne's, especially with Duncan.

"Stop touching everything!" I yank him by the arm and pull him closer. "Let me look at the list for a minute, would ya?"

Duncan starts whispering into his hand. "Batman…Batman, you there?"

"Oh, don't start, please," I say.

"I'm here, Robin," he says in a deeper voice.

"Keep it down!" I hiss. I can feel people staring. "Here, you push the cart. Pretend it's the Batmobile."

Duncan smiles, then speaks into his hand, "We're leaving the Batcave. Hold on."

He makes a weird swishing noise to go along with the movement of the cart. I walk in front of him, trying to tune out his noises. Duncan follows me through the aisles, bumping into things every once in a while.

Just as we turn into the third aisle, he rams the cart into my heels. "Oww!" I yell. "Would you watch it!"

"You stopped."

"Let me push the cart past this crazy lineup," I say. I wonder what's going on. Then I notice the sign that reads, *Sidney Crosby will be signing autographs today until noon.*

I think about joining the line. But when Duncan's whispers turn into a loud argument between Batman and the Joker, I know we can't do it. I shove the cart toward the lightbulb section.

"Hey, Max!"

I turn around. Ian is almost at the front of the line. "Can you believe it?" He pulls a puck from his pocket. "I'm going to get it signed."

"Cool…"

"Have you talked to your mom about playing yet?"

"Not yet," I say. "I keep waiting for the right moment, but it never seems to come."

"Just ask her, would ya!" Ian jabs me in the arm. "Hey, I'll get something signed for you if you want."

I dig into my pocket and pull out the money Mom gave me and a ten-dollar bill from shoveling Mr. Cooper's driveway. "I don't have anything."

The line starts moving. "Okay, man. I'll see if he has a flyer or something."

"Thanks." I turn to make sure Duncan isn't getting into anything. A sick feeling makes my stomach lurch.

He's gone.

Chapter Three

Where *is* he?

I whirl the cart around.

"Did you see the tall boy I was with?" I ask a man standing in the lineup for Sidney Crosby. "He was probably talking to himself."

"Sorry, can't say I did. Why don't you ask—"

I don't wait for him to finish. I push the cart past all the people and glance down each aisle as I head to the other end of the store.

Nothing.

My last hope is the cereal aisle. Duncan usually gets obsessed with a new brand.

He's not there.

I'm starting to freak. What am I going to tell Mom? My heart pounds in my chest like it does when I'm going in for a goal. I'm almost running now. The electronics section is at the end of the row. And then it hits me. He's probably in the movie section.

I zoom around the corner and, sure enough, Duncan is standing in front of the big TV screen. The latest Spider-Man movie is playing, and he is glued to it— and I mean glued. If he was any closer, he'd be hugging the TV.

I'm relieved to see him, but at the same time I'm really ticked off. I wasn't talking to Ian for that long.

"Duncan, you scared me," I say. "You can't run off like that!"

"I'm not Duncan, I'm Spider-Man!"

"I don't care who you are! We've got to go."

"But I want to watch." He points at the screen.

"You can watch one when we get home. Come on." I pull on his arm.

"No!"

"Stop embarrassing me," I whisper. "Let's go!"

I grab the cart and drag him out of the electronics section.

Bleep, bleep, bleep. The alarm goes off as soon as we walk through the area.

"Hang on there!" One of Bucky Dwayne's security guys runs over.

"I think you have something that hasn't been paid for."

Duncan has a video in his hands. *Great!*

"Oh, sorry, this is not what it looks like," I say to the guy. "Duncan, you've got to give the movie back."

"But I want it," he wails.

"You've got a whole bunch at home. Come on, give it to me." I try yanking it out of his hands.

"No!" Duncan says, clutching it to his chest. "I'm in charge."

People are staring at us. If Duncan was little, they would ignore us, but a teenager having a tantrum like this is not a common sight. Bucky Dwayne's security guy doesn't know what to do. We're now the Saturday entertainment.

"Oh, forget it…I'll just pay for it!" I grab Duncan by the sleeve and walk over to the cashier in the electronics department.

"Can I pay for the rest of the stuff in my cart too?" I ask the cashier.

"Sure, that's fine," she says.

"I hope you're happy!" I glare at Duncan.

"I like this movie," Duncan tells the cashier.

"Well, let me scan it, hon." She leans over the counter while Duncan holds it for her. She totals everything up. "That will be forty-five dollars and fifty-seven cents."

I reach into my pocket and pull out the money, I start counting. A sick feeling twists my stomach around. Even with my own money I'm short eight bucks.

"Ah…I think I have to put something back," I say quietly.

"Excuse me?"

"I don't have enough," I say a little louder.

"Supervisor to electronics," she announces over the loudspeaker.

"You've got to be kidding me," a familiar voice moans from the back of the line. "What's the holdup?"

I stand there like a complete loser, trying to ignore Cody Shanks.

"Hey, bonehead," Cody jeers. "Are you going to answer me?"

I can't bring myself to turn around. My face turns a thousand shades of red.

"You can go to the next department," the cashier says to him. "Someone will help you there."

"Whatever," Cody grunts.

"He needs to strengthen his patience muscle," the cashier whispers. "Don't you think?"

"Yeah, something like that," I say.

On the bus ride home, Duncan sits in his favorite spot behind the driver. He has a big smile on his face as he says hello to everyone who gets on the bus. I lean my head against the window as we fly along the Bedford Highway.

It's hard to stay mad at him.

The next stop is ours. I make my way toward the front of the bus. "You can pull the bell now," I say to Duncan. "But just once, okay?"

Duncan nods. "Just once." He reaches up and yanks the rope. We've been practicing this for the last few months. The first couple of times, Duncan went crazy with the bell ringing. Today it goes off without a hitch.

"Good job." I reach over to steady him as he stands up.

"Thank you, bus driver," Duncan says before getting off.

"See you later, boys."

We walk up the hill in silence. As I unlock the back door, I say, "We'd better be quiet okay? Mom is probably still sleeping."

"She likes her bed," Duncan says.

"Yeah, I know what you mean."

I dump the shopping bags on the

kitchen table. I notice a flyer for Sidney Crosby. If Dad had been alive, he would have made sure I got to meet him. Mom doesn't have a clue who's who in the hockey world. I tear up the flyer and shove it in the garbage. The lid slams shut with a bang.

I hear voices coming from Mom's room upstairs. I thought for sure she'd still be sleeping. I knock on her door before sticking my head in. "You up?"

"Oh! You're back. I couldn't sleep, so I thought I'd just…"

I glance over at the TV. She's been watching home movies. My stomach tightens as I catch a glimpse of Dad. He's laughing and wading into the water with Duncan in his arms. I sit down on the bed.

"Wasn't Duncan precious?" She reaches for a box of tissues and blows her nose.

"Sometimes I wonder what he'd be like now if he hadn't had that awful fever."

"Mom, don't."

"Daddy and I were so worried he wasn't going to make it."

"Why don't I turn the lights on?" I ask.

"They're burnt out," she says. "I don't know what's wrong with them. One burnt out last night and the other went this morning. Oh, look at Daddy." She points to the TV.

"I'll go get the lightbulbs." I would do anything to get out of that room. I find it hard to hear Dad's voice. It makes me miss him more than I already do. Besides, I can't stand seeing Mom cry.

I dump the groceries onto the kitchen table.

No lightbulbs.

Why did this have to happen on the day she's crying over home movies?

I head back upstairs.

"Oh, Max, honestly. I thought the list was pretty straightforward!" Mom says when I tell her I didn't buy lightbulbs.

"You're not being quiet," Duncan butts in. He's standing in the doorway. "Remember, Max? You said to be quiet."

"It's okay, Duncan," Mom says. "I couldn't sleep."

"I like my new movie," he says in a deep voice. "Thank you, Max."

She looks at me. "Is that why you didn't get the lightbulbs, Max? You can't give in every time he wants something. You know that."

"You don't understand what happened!" I plead.

She yanks the sheets off her bed. "All I wanted was lightbulbs. Was that too much to ask?"

She thumps around her bedroom picking things up. "I don't have the patience for this, Max." Her voice is shaky.

Duncan's smile fades. He turns to leave, and then he notices Dad on the TV. "I want to talk to him. I want to see him *now*." He walks over to the TV and starts hitting the top of it.

"Duncan, you can't, sweetheart. It's only a movie." She puts her arm around him and rests her head on his shoulder. "I know it's hard. We all miss him."

"Dad's not grumpy like you," Duncan says.

Mom is fighting back tears.

"Come on, Duncan," I say. "Let's leave her alone."

I turn on another movie for Duncan, hoping it will take his mind off Dad. Back in my room I flop onto my bed and pound my fists into the pillow.

Chapter Four

No one answers the phone. On the fourth ring, I roll off my bed and search for it. I pitch several hockey magazines off my desk before I find it.

"Hello?"

"Hey!" Ian says. "The puck is signed. You should see his signature, Max. It's crazy. Oh, and I got something for you too."

"You did?" I sit on the edge of my bed listening to him.

"Yeah, Sidney had stuff on his table for free," says Ian. "I grabbed you a poster."

"Thanks, Ian."

"No problem. Hey, a bunch of us are going to practice on the pond. Do you want to come?"

"Um, I'll see if I can. Call you back, okay?"

I head downstairs. Mom is washing dishes, and Duncan is eating a sandwich.

"Um, I'm sorry about the lightbulbs," I mumble.

She turns to face me and sighs. "I'm sorry too. I shouldn't have reacted the way I did. I'm just so…"

"It's okay. Um, I was wondering if I could go skate on the pond with Ian."

"I want to come too," Duncan says with his mouth full.

"No way, Duncan!" I say. "You'll be bored in two seconds."

"You know, honey, that would be a big help. I do need to sleep, or I won't be able to function." Mom wipes her hands on the dishtowel.

"Are you serious? I can't keep him busy while I'm skating!"

"I'm sure the puck leaves the pond every now and then. It certainly did when you and Daddy played. Duncan could collect them. I'll make some hot chocolate for him. What do you think?"

I don't know why she bothers asking. It's not like I have a choice. "Fine!" I shove the chair into the table and glare at Duncan.

Ian and the others are on the pond when we finally arrive. It took forever to get out the door. I couldn't find one of my hockey gloves. Duncan sat in the kitchen with his hat, mitts and winter coat on for a good twenty minutes while I searched the house.

"Took you long enough!" Ian yells. He skates over and stops within inches of the edge of the pond.

"He skates fast," Duncan says. Then he walks off to investigate something in the snow.

"Why is he here?" Ian whispers.

"Don't ask!" I say.

"What's he going to do?" Ian asks.

"Get the pucks for us." I roll my eyes. "Mom's idea."

Duncan comes back and sits down on the bench.

"So...I hear you're going to be the puck getter?" Ian says, leaning on his hockey stick.

"Yes, I am!" Duncan says in one of his deep voices. "Max, I'm going to be the puck getter."

"I know." I finish tying up my skates, pull the thermos out and hand it to him.

"Here's your hot chocolate. Careful—it's hot."

"I like hot chocolate," Duncan says and then blows on it.

I glide onto the pond. I feel like I'm floating as my skates cut through the ice. I throw my boots on top of the boot pile that we use as a net and join the rest of the guys.

I skate around the pond a few times to warm up. The cold air stings my cheeks. I can't help but smile. It feels good to be skating. It's like Dad is right with me.

Duncan seems fine sitting on the bench drinking his hot chocolate. Maybe Mom was right.

"Can we play?" asks a familiar voice.

I whirl around. Oh, man! Twice in one day. Cody stands at the edge of the pond with four of his friends. I don't recognize any of them.

Ian looks at me. I shrug my shoulders. If I say no, I'll never hear the end of it.

If I say yes, maybe he'll forget about the lineup today. I nod.

"Yeah, all right," Ian says. "We can split up—five on five."

Within a few minutes we're scrambling to get the puck. Ian takes a wild shot. The puck flies off the ice and lands on the path.

"Duncan! Can you get that?" I yell over to him.

"Yes, I can." He walks quickly, spilling his hot chocolate along the way. "I found it! I found it!"

"Who's that?" one of Cody's friends asks.

"My brother." I don't look at the guy.

"Look at him go," Cody says. He and his friends laugh. "What a dork."

"Put your hot chocolate down and throw the puck," I yell, pretending Cody's laughter isn't punching me in the stomach.

Duncan throws the puck, but it doesn't reach the pond. He retrieves it and throws it again. This time it lands near the edge.

"I'm a good puck getter!" Duncan says proudly.

I skate over and scoop it up.

"Can we get this game going?" Cody bellows.

Duncan paces by the side of the pond waiting for the next puck.

"Over here, Max!" Ian yells.

I pass Ian the puck and then skate toward the net.

"Hey, watch it!" Cody says, after I cut in front of him.

"*You* watch it!" I snap.

"Ian! Over here!" I yell. He passes me the puck, and I fly up the ice and slam it into the net. The boots fly all over the place.

"Nice one!" Ian yells. He skates over, and we smack our sticks together.

Ian and I take charge of the puck for the entire game, playing like we're on the

Olympic team. We skate circles around Cody and his friends, which really ticks them off. During the second period, we're five goals ahead when Ian scores a goal and lands in the net with the puck, taking the goalie down with him. This is Ian's trademark move.

"Hey! What are you doing?" yells Cody.

I turn to see what Cody is complaining about.

"He's got my boots!" Cody yells.

Duncan has a pair of boots in his arms. The other team's net is gone. All the boots are in one big straight line across the pond.

Chapter Five

I zoom toward the line of boots. "Duncan! What are you *doing*?"

He looks at me like I'm from Mars.

"It's our net, Duncan!" I grab the boots from his arms and throw them onto the ice. "They're *supposed* to be in a pile!"

"Oh, your net." Duncan's face falls.

"Can we get this game going? This isn't friggin' *Sesame Street*," Cody yells.

He and his friends lean on their sticks, laughing. Why did I agree to let them play?

"Duncan, grab some boots and throw them into the middle." I start whacking boots with my stick.

I just want to play hockey.

Duncan picks the boots up one at a time and carefully places them onto the pile. I know it's killing him to leave the boots in a mess. As he grabs the last one, he slips on the ice.

Smack! The sound echoes across the pond. A small crack appears in the ice where Duncan lands.

I race over and kneel next to him. Duncan looks up with tears in his eyes. "It hurts, it hurts!" He's holding his right arm.

"Okay, I won't touch it."

Ian skates over. "Is he okay?"

"His arm hurts. Can you help me get him up?"

"Sure." Ian drops his stick.

Duncan doesn't make it easy for us. He sits there like deadweight.

Ian and I are on either side of him, trying to grab hold of him without touching his sore arm.

"Okay—you got him, Ian?"

"Yup. We're going to get you up there, Puck Getter," Ian says.

"I'm not Puck Getter, I'm Spider-Man."

"Okay, Spider-Man…on the count of three, we're going to lift you. One—two—three! Oh, man," Ian groans. "You're heavy!"

Duncan wails, "My arm, my arm!"

"You're not going to die, okay?" I say. Once we have him standing, I brush snow off his jacket.

"This is a waste of time!" Cody hollers. "When are we going to get this game going?"

"My arm hurts," says Duncan.

"Yeah. I know, Duncan." I'm so mad inside, I could scream. "I gotta go." I can't look at Ian when I say the words. I grab my boots from the pile and make my way to the side of the pond.

"What are you doing?" Cody yells.

"We're going home," I bark. "What's it *look* like?"

"Losers!"

"What is his problem?" I mutter under my breath.

"He's mean," Duncan answers.

It always amazes me how in some ways Duncan can be completely clueless, and in others so smart.

"*Pst...Pst...*"

"Duncan, knock it off, would ya?"

"*Pst...Pst...*" He completely ignores me.

It becomes obvious why he's making the noises. With his good hand, he's got his fingers spread far apart as he directs his spiderweb toward Cody.

"I'm going to wrap him in my web. He's a bad guy."

Before I can say another word, Duncan bolts from the bench and heads onto the ice.

The guys have started passing the puck around, but Duncan doesn't seem to care. He gets right in front of Cody.

"Duncan, stop!" I yell as I scramble after him, wearing one boot and one skate.

"I've got you!" Duncan yells. He flings his good arm toward Cody.

"Get him away from me," Cody yells as he pushes his hands out in front of his face.

"Ian, *grab* him!" I yell.

Ian skates toward Duncan.

Cody drops his stick. He looks like he's ready to punch Duncan. His thick brain doesn't have the sense to skate away. He could do laps around Duncan. All he has to do is skate away.

Cody's friends stand watching like a bunch of doorknobs.

"Leave him alone," I scream. "He's not going to hurt you!"

"Get this *freak* away from me!" Cody yells.

Ian tries to pull Duncan away, but Duncan yanks free and plows into Cody, pushing him onto the ice. Cody's friends laugh.

Cody scrambles to his feet with his fists punching the air. I can barely keep my balance as I hobble and slide over to Duncan. I manage to get there in time to intercept Cody's fist.

Smack!

He hits me so hard, I fall backward and land butt-first on the ice. I sit there for a few seconds. My head pounds, and my right eye feels like it's going to pop out.

Cody spits at me. His goober lands with a big *splat* beside my feet. "If that freak comes near me again, he'll get it good." Then he kicks my skate to get his point across.

If my head wasn't spinning so badly, I'd punch him back. Instead I pull myself to my feet and stagger off the ice.

Ian is sitting on the bench with Duncan by the time I make if off the pond.

"My arm hurts," Duncan whimpers.

"Well, if you hadn't gone after Cody, you'd be fine!" I hiss. I drop down beside him and take off my other skate. Cody messes around with the puck as if nothing happened.

I can tell Ian feels bad, but he doesn't know what to say. What is there to say? Sorry your brother messed things up again? Sorry you have no life? He says, "I'll come over afterward."

I sling my skates over my shoulder. "Let's go, Duncan."

I lead the way through the path. Every now and then, Duncan whispers to himself.

"You're strong, Spider-Man. You can fix this," followed by, "Ohhhh, my arm hurts!"

My eye throbs. I try to ignore it.

When we arrive home, our back door is locked. Mom has a habit of bolting it shut when we leave, even if she's home. I reach into my pocket for the key. It's not there. I drop my hockey gear and search all my pockets—nothing. Sighing, I ring the doorbell and wait. Nothing.

I ring it again. And we wait.

Nothing—a big fat nothing.

Chapter Six

"Stay here, Duncan. I'll go check Dad's workshop for the spare. I'll be right back." I trudge through the snow in the backyard. I haven't been in Dad's little shed for a while. The smell of wood and sawdust tickles my nose and reminds me of Dad. I used to love hanging out with him. I used to watch for hours as he built things out of wood. It was our special thing, that and playing hockey. My fingers fumble on the ledge where the key used to be.

Zippo—not a thing.

I shut the door and glance up at Mom's window. The curtains are closed. I start yelling, "Mom! Open up. We're locked out!" I stare at the curtains, hoping to see her open them. I grab a snowball and toss it near her window. It splats on the side of the house. But it doesn't do any good—the curtains don't move.

"How can she not hear us?" I mutter.

"She's not home," Duncan says.

"Maybe you're right. Come on, let's go over to Mr. Cooper's."

Duncan follows me, complaining how hungry he is. We cut through the rosebushes and ring the back doorbell.

"We're locked out," I announce when Mr. Cooper opens the door.

"My arm hurts," Duncan adds.

"Your arm hurts, and you're locked out. Not a good combination. Come on in."

The warmth from Mr. Cooper's woodstove makes my face tingle. I take off my mitts.

"Looks like you two were in a bit of a wrestling match. Your eye looks mighty sore there, Max."

"I was fighting," Duncan says in a deep voice.

"You were not!" I roll my eyes. "We both fell on the pond." I don't want to tell Mr. Cooper what happened. He might tell Mom.

"Sounds like you ran into a patch of bad luck." Mr. Cooper rummages around in a kitchen drawer. "Here we go. I knew I had one." He dangles a spare set of keys.

"Thanks," I say. I take them and turn toward the back door.

"My arm hurts," Duncan complains.

"Why don't I have a look at it?" Mr. Cooper says as he pulls out a chair. "Come have a seat, Duncan, or are you Spider-Man today?"

"I'm Spider-Man," he answers quietly.

Mr. Cooper tries to touch his arm.

"Oweeee!" Duncan yells.

"Okay there. Let's not get our knickers in a knot, Spider-Man." Mr. Cooper gets up and pulls a first-aid kit out of a cupboard. "I reckon I have a Spider-Man sling for you."

"You do?" Duncan's eyes light up.

"I sure do." He unwraps a beige triangle bandage. "I'm going to have to touch your arm, but I promise I'll be as gentle as possible."

Duncan sits still while Mr. Cooper slips the sling on his arm. "I like you," Duncan whispers.

"Well, I like you too. That should do the trick until your mom gets home."

"I'm hungry," Duncan says.

"Well, there's nothing like telling a feller how it really is." Mr. Cooper chuckles. "What would you like to eat?"

"That's okay, Mr. Cooper. I'll make him something when we get home. Come on, let's go, Duncan. Thanks for the key."

"No worries, Max. I'm always here."

At home, I check my eye out in the bathroom mirror. It's turning different shades of red and blue.

My first black eye.

Chapter Seven

"I'm hungry," Duncan says from the kitchen.

"Just give me a minute," I holler. When I come back into the kitchen, Duncan rests his head on the table and cradles his arm. I can tell he's in a lot of pain. I grab a pot and start making macaroni and cheese. "Hopefully Mom will be back any minute so we can get your arm checked out," I say. Duncan doesn't answer me.

The doorbell rings just as Duncan is eating his last bite. Ian stands on the step with his hockey gear.

"That was quick," I say. "I thought you were going to stay and play?"

"Cody slapped every puck we had into the woods. We couldn't find them. He was being such a jerk no one wanted to stick around. Are you going to let me in or what?"

"Yeah…yeah, come on in."

Ian flings his boots off and leaves them in a heap by the back door. When he sees Duncan, he says, "We sure could have used you at the pond."

"I hurt my arm," Duncan mumbles.

"Want something to eat, Ian?" I ask.

"Yeah, I'm starving," says Ian.

"Sandwich okay?"

"Yeah, sounds good."

I pull out ingredients from the meat tray and dump them on the counter. Ian grabs the bread, and we make monster-sized layered sandwiches.

"Hey, look at this." Ian picks up the cheese-slice package and reads the back. "*Kids Help Phone. 1-800 blah blah blah.* That's a weird place to put that."

"Let me see." I grab the package. "You're right. That is weird."

"Yeah," Ian says with a mouthful. "Can you imagine calling them and saying, I'm having trouble making my cheese sandwich. Can you help me?"

We laugh so hard that I don't hear Mom come into the kitchen. Her hair is a mess of tangles, and her makeup is smeared underneath her eyes.

"Oh no! What happened to Duncan?"

"I was fighting," Duncan says in a low voice.

"You were what?" She then looks at me. "Oh my goodness! What happened to your eye?"

"He wasn't fighting," I snap. "He slipped on the ice! And my eye, well—"

"Spider-Man was fighting!" Duncan pounds his good fist onto the table. "I got him in my web!"

"Okay, Duncan, settle down. It sounds like—"

"My arm hurts!" says Duncan.

Mom sits down next to him. "Let's have a look."

"Don't touch it!" Duncan orders. "Only Spider-Man can."

"This isn't the time to fool around, Duncan."

"I think it might be sprained," I say. "Mr. Cooper put the sling on."

"Mr. Cooper?"

"Yeah, we were locked out. I forgot my key."

"Oh, Max…Why didn't you ring the doorbell?"

"I did! For, like, five minutes!" I say.

"Oh. I didn't hear it." Her face falls.

"My arm hurts!" Duncan wails.

"I *know,* Duncan. So, what happened to your eye, Max?" Mom looks right at me.

"I'll tell you later," I say.

"We were fighting," Duncan says.

"For Pete's sake. What is going on?" Tears fill her eyes.

"Nothing, Mom. It's like I said. We fell on the ice."

She looks at the clock. "Oh great— the clinic closes in less than an hour. Look at me! I'm a mess. I can't see the doctor like this."

"You don't look all that bad, Mrs. O'Neil," Ian says.

I cringe. I can't even look at her. I stare at my feet. I know Ian is trying to help. The old Mom would have smiled at Ian's attempt to say something nice. Ian forgets we're dealing with the new Mrs. O'Neil—the one who's lost her sense of humor and everything else that used to make her fun.

"Does your mother know you're here, Ian?" she asks.

"I, er, no. She thinks I'm on the pond. I came to see how Duncan was."

"Perhaps you should go, Ian," says Mom.

"But he just got here!" I say.

"Max. Not today. I'll be down in five minutes, Duncan."

"Your mom is kind of freaked out. Do you think she's mad at us?" Ian asks at the back door.

"Wouldn't be anything new. She's always mad now, and everything that goes wrong is my fault!"

Chapter Eight

Mom sits at the kitchen table and stares me down. "Okay, what happened at the pond? Duncan talked nonstop about it to Dr. Graham. Just tell me straight up. I don't have the energy for games," she says.

I lean against the fridge with my arms folded. I know she's not going to let up until I give her something.

So I tell her what happened—except the part where Cody punched me. I make it sound like Duncan bumped me when he fell. There's no way I'm telling her how Cody treated Duncan. I'll never be allowed to go to the pond again if I tell her what really happened.

"Oh, Max, I shouldn't have made you take him." She rests her head in her hands. "I can't do this anymore," she whispers. "I just can't…"

I don't know what to say. Mouse jumps down from the window ledge with a thud and wraps his body in between my legs. I can feel his purring. I bend down to pick him up, but the phone rings, so I leave him on the ground.

"I don't want to talk to anyone. Take a message," she says.

"Hello? Um…just a sec." I cover the receiver with my hand and whisper, "It's Maggie."

Mom shakes her head. "Not now."

Mom and Maggie have been friends since grade three, but even Maggie can't help her right now.

"I can't keep telling her you're working! Come on, Mom."

She gives me a look that says, *Don't you dare.*

I glare at her as I lie. "She's still sleeping, Maggie."

"Don't you look at me like that," she says when I hang up. "You have no idea what I'm going through." She brushes past me and heads upstairs. "Get some frozen peas on that eye of yours."

I slam a cupboard shut and stomp around the kitchen. "I miss him too! Did you ever think about that?" I yell. "Of course not! You're too busy crying and hiding in your bedroom!"

I hear Mom's bedroom door slam. Now I've done it. Sighing, I decide to clean up my mess so she won't have something else to be mad at me for.

The last thing I put away is the cheese-slice package. I stare at the ad for the Kids Help Phone. I wonder how many kids see the number and want to call but never do.

I grab the peas from the freezer and plunk myself down on the sofa.

I put my feet on the coffee table and rest my head against the back of the sofa. The cold peas feel good on my eye. They numb my thoughts for a few minutes.

"What you need is a good laugh," Ian says after school the next day. "Look and learn."

He flops down on my bed, tucks his legs into his chest and holds them in place with his arms. His butt sticks up in the air. "Okay, light the match when I tell you, and hold it close to my butt. Just don't light my jeans on fire."

"You're nuts, you know. Mom will kill me if she finds out."

"Okay…here it comes!" Ian yells, ignoring me.

I frantically light the match and hold it near Ian's bum. One loud rip-roaring fart thunders out of him.

Braaaaoooooooommmmm.

A big blue flame shoots out from Ian's butt with a *pfft* sound.

"Wow! Did you see that?" I jump back, laughing my head off.

"No, but I felt it. You had the match too close." Ian grins from ear to ear.

"That was way cool," I say.

"You want to try now?" Ian asks.

"Sure." I lie on the bed and tuck my knees into my chest just like Ian. "This is too funny."

Ian is already positioned, ready to strike the match. I hold my breath and try to squeeze one out.

"Can't do anything," I say. I try again. "Still nothing."

"No worries. Thunder Bum to the rescue. Push over."

Just as Ian's about to let another one rip, I glance over at my bedroom door. I'd forgotten to close it.

"Okay, I'm ready to *blow*. Light it! Light it!" Ian yells.

I fumble with the matches. I get one lit just in time.

Brrrrrroookkaaapppoffft.

"Whoa! That was the best one yet!" I yell.

Duncan comes barreling in with his Spider-Man cup full of water. Before I have time to stop him, he throws it on Ian.

"Hey, what are you doing?" Ian yells.

"Your bum was on fire," Duncan says in a low shaky voice.

"It's okay, Duncan. Ian's not hurt. We were just doing blue darts." I turn my head and plug my nose—to stop myself from laughing.

But when Duncan says, "You look like you peed your pants," I lose it.

"You think it's funny, do you?" Ian says, standing with his hands on his hips and a wet stain on the crotch of his pants.

"I like you, Ian," Duncan says, pointing to him.

"You have a weird way of showing it," Ian says, wiping at his pants.

"Max, Ian's funny," Duncan says. Then he leaves my room.

"Man, he appears out of nowhere, doesn't he?" Ian says.

"Yeah, sorry about that." I open up my drawer. "Here, try these." I throw him a pair of jeans.

After Ian changes, he flops down on the bed and picks up a hockey magazine. "Hey, what are you going to do about the game on Friday?"

"Haven't a clue—I'm still working on it."

Chapter Nine

"Ian's bum was on fire," Duncan announces at supper.

Oh, great.

Mom drops her fork and looks back and forth between the two of us.

"Max, what is Duncan talking about?"

"It was nothing." I smirk, remembering how funny it was.

"I put his bum fire out," Duncan says, after pushing his plate away.

"Will someone tell me what's going on?"

"It was no big deal, Mom. Ian came over today, and we were fooling around in my room. He was showing me how to do blue darts."

"What in heaven's name are blue darts?"

"Bums blow out fire," Duncan says, as he gets up to leave the table.

I glare at Duncan's back.

"Let me get this straight, you were playing with matches?"

"Sort of, but we were really careful."

"Good lord, Max! What has got into you? You could have started a fire. This isn't like you at all." Her voice quivers. "It's Ian—isn't it? He's not to be here when I'm not home."

"Mom! That's not fair. I'm not stupid. I wasn't going to burn down the house by lighting a few dumb farts."

I stand up and shove my chair into the table. "This sucks. I'm always looking after Duncan! I never get to play hockey. Ever since Dad died, I have to do everything!"

There.

I'd said it.

My whole body is clenched tight, waiting for her to say something.

"What do you expect me to do?" she finally says. "Do you think I like leaving you alone all the time with Duncan?" Her voice cracks. She scrunches up the napkins and gathers the rest of the dishes. "I'm still trying to figure things out, Max. We all have to do our bit."

"I am doing my bit!"

She stands at the kitchen sink with her back toward me, bracing her hands on the counter. "Max, please…"

"No, Mom, I'm not finished. I'm always late for school because of Duncan. I can't play hockey like I used to, because I have to look after him. He blabs off at the mouth to my friends and Mr. Cooper. He acts so retarded. I hate it." Just as the words blast out of my mouth, Duncan comes into the kitchen with his hands covering his ears.

"You're hurting my ears," he says.

"I…"

"It's okay, Duncan. He didn't mean it. Did you, Max?"

The trouble was, I did mean it.

I just didn't mean for Duncan to hear me.

"Max! Say you're sorry," Mom says.

I look at Duncan. "Sorry," I mutter.

I flop down on my bed and dial Ian's number.

"Hey, what's wrong? You sound bummed out," Ian asks.

"Mom and I got in a big fight."

"Not again—what was it this time?"

"Take a wild guess," I say.

"Not the blue darts?"

"Yup. Duncan flapped his lips about it at supper."

"Oh, man—that's a bummer. Hey, get it? Bummer?" Ian laughs.

"Yeah, well, Mom's so mad at me right now, I don't think I'm going to be able to skate on Friday."

"You have to play," Ian says.

I stare at my big toe poking out of a hole in my sock. "Believe me, I want to!"

Braaap. Ian lets out a big loud burp. "Okay, so we know bringing Duncan to the pond won't work."

"Duh!" I say as I take off my socks.

"Couldn't you just set him up with a long movie? He'd never even know you were gone."

I bunch my socks in a ball and pitch them to the other end of the room. "Don't think I haven't thought about that. But if anything happened, Mom would lose it."

I stand up and look out my window. Snow swirls around outside. Every once in a while it makes a pinging sound on the window.

"Hey! I've got it," Ian says.

"What?"

"Why don't you ask Lilly? She's Duncan's school buddy this month. She's always telling my mom that she really likes him. I bet if we paid her five bucks, she'd do it. You could put a movie on before you leave. You'd be back before your mom gets home. No one would ever know."

"You're forgetting about Duncan's big mouth!"

"What if we get Lilly to come *after* you get his movie on?"

"Hmmm. That might work. Will you call her?"

"Sure."

"I better go." Just as I'm about to hang up, I say, "Hey, Ian?"

"Yeah?"

"Thanks."

"Forget about it." He lets out another burp and then hangs up.

At bedtime I can't sleep. The day's events play over and over in my head. I turn my light on and head downstairs for a snack. When I slip past Duncan's room, I notice the TV is still on. He looks fast asleep. I tiptoe in and turn it off.

"I'm still watching," comes a voice from underneath the blankets.

"Jeez, you scared me!" I whirl around. "Don't do that to me!" I turn the TV back on and close the door.

I sit down at the kitchen table with a bowl of cereal. The hum of the fridge and the *tick-tock* of the kitchen clock keep me company. Everything is fine until I think of Mom and what she was

saying earlier. *I can't do this anymore...*
My stomach tightens, and I've lost my
appetite. What did she mean by that?
And then I remember all the stuff I said
to her. I'm just like Duncan—blurting
out things I should keep inside.

Chapter Ten

The next morning I grab the money jar from the cupboard and dump loose change onto the counter. There's enough for my lunch. Duncan is a different story. The only sandwich he'll eat is cheese slices with mayonnaise and ketchup. It's gross when the ketchup drips out the sides, but Duncan loves them. I grab the last two cheese slices, throw the wrappers in the garbage and slap it together.

Mouse slips out the back door when we leave for school. When we pass Mr. Cooper's house, he's picking up his morning paper from the middle of his driveway. We stop to say hi.

He stands up and gives his pants a yank. "Hi, Max. Hey there, Spider-Man. How's your arm?"

Duncan's face beams when Mr. Cooper calls him Spider-Man. He then blows it by saying, "I saw your bum. You need a belt."

I feel my face get red. Mr. Cooper acts as though he doesn't hear Duncan. "I hope that shiner of an eye doesn't hurt too badly there, Max."

"Nah, it's alright," I say.

When we're out of earshot, I say, "Jeez, Duncan, you don't have to say everything you're thinking."

When we get to the path that leads through the woods, I take a different route. It's a few minutes longer, which is why we never use it.

But I have to now. I can't take the chance we'll run into Cody.

Duncan follows me and then stops a few feet into it. "This isn't my path." He turns around to go back.

"We're trying out a new one today," I say. "Come on. It will be fun. I promise."

Duncan looks at me like I've got two heads. He starts walking back. I have to think of something quick. If only I could tell him this is for his own good, but he won't understand. So I do the only thing I can think of.

"Batman," I say into my hand like *he* normally does. "We're on an adventure. Come on, there's no time to waste."

Duncan grins and says, "Okay, Robin. I'm coming."

We talk back and forth the entire time. In a weird way, it's fun—and it takes my mind off what might happen if we run into Cody.

Ian comes up to my locker before music class with a big grin on his face. "Lilly will do it!"

"She will?" I ask.

"I be the man. You can thank me later. I'm late for science. Gotta go."

On the way to music class, I notice Lilly and Duncan taking papers to the office. "Hi, Max," she says when I get closer.

"That's my brother," Duncan says pointing toward me.

Lilly smiles.

"Is Lilly your buddy this month?" I ask Duncan.

"She's Mary Jane," Duncan says and then giggles. "She's my girlfriend."

"He's a riot," she whispers. "I guess we'll talk later about things."

"I'm not a riot. I'm Spider-Man." He stretches his hand out and spreads his fingers.

"You didn't tell Lilly that you have supersonic hearing did you, Spider-Man?" I say.

"Lilly, I have supersonic hearing," says Duncan.

"Let's move it along." Mr. G., the music teacher, says from the doorway of music class. The squeaking and squawking of clarinets and trumpets warming up drifts into the hallway.

"That's too loud," Duncan says, covering his ears as they walk past.

"I wish I could do that too, Duncan." Mr. G. smiles and then closes the door behind me.

After music, I head back to my locker. As I'm reaching for my math book, I feel someone standing beside me.

I hold my breath when I recognize Cody's red sneakers below my locker.

"I better not see your brother on the pond again!" he hisses. Then he shoves me into my locker.

Wham!

He leans in close. "You hear me!" His breath makes me want to throw up.

I rub my arm as I watch Cody saunter down the hall with his pants hanging down so low it looks like his butt is at his ankles.

Chapter Eleven

At supper, I fiddle with my food while Duncan talks nonstop about Mary Jane.

"Who's Mary Jane?" Mom asks.

"Mary Jane is my girlfriend," Duncan says in his deepest voice.

"Max? Do you know Mary Jane?"

I hear her, but I'm stuck in my brain, thinking about Cody and what he might do to me next.

"Max?"

"*What*? She's from one of his stupid movies," I snap. "If you knew anything, you'd know she's Peter Parker's girlfriend!"

"You don't need to be rude."

I didn't mean to snap at her, but this talk about Mary Jane is making me think about Lilly babysitting on Friday. Maybe it's not a good idea.

"I like you, Mom," Duncan says. He takes his dishes to the sink and then announces, "I'm going to watch my movies."

"Thanks for telling me," she says. "And I like you too."

Now I feel rotten. I can't go behind Mom's back. Besides, Duncan will blow it one way or another. Maybe I should ask her one last time just in case she says yes.

"Um, about Friday..." I clear my throat. "I was wondering if I can play in the hockey game. It's super important. They really need me."

Mom takes an unusually deep breath and then sighs. I wait for her to say something. Finally she says, "Okay…let me see what I can do."

Later that night I call Ian.

"I can play!" I say.

"You *can*?" asks Ian.

"Yup. And I won't have Duncan either. Mom's going to meet him at school, so I don't even have to walk him home. Will you tell Lilly I don't need her?"

Ian lets out a humongous burp. *Braaaaaaaaaaaaaap!*

"I'll take that as a yes." I laugh.

"We're going to have a blast," says Ian.

The next morning I lug my hockey gear to the school. The ice on the pond glistens in the morning sunlight. I can't wait to play this afternoon. It's going to be sweet. The day ticks by like it's never going to end. Every time I glance at the clock, it has barely moved. When the last bell finally rings, I bolt down the hall and collide with Miss Thorne, the guidance counselor.

"You're in a big hurry, aren't you?" she asks.

"Sorry, Miss Thorne."

"Let's keep it to a walking pace, please," she says, smiling.

Ian is waiting by my locker. "Come on, man. I want to get to the pond to warm up."

"I need to get Duncan," I say, shoving books in my locker. "Mom should be waiting outside, and then we can go."

When I get to Duncan's room, he's talking to the class pet hamster.

"Come on. We've got to go," I say.

Instead of holding things up, as usual, he says, "Bye, Snuggles. See you tomorrow."

"That was quick," Ian says.

"I think he's happy Mom's picking him up."

Outside, I scan the parking lot for Mom's car. It's not there. I run down the steps to look around the side of the school.

Nothing.

Ian glances at his watch. "Do you think she forgot?"

"No," I snap. "She knew it was important."

"I'm just saying. You know, what with how she's been acting—"

"I want to go home," Duncan says and heads down the steps.

"Wait!" I stop him at the bottom. "Mom will be here any minute." I stare at the parking lot, willing her to appear. One by one, cars pull in and pick their kids up, but none of them are for us.

Ian looks at his watch again. "I gotta go, man. I'll meet you there, okay?"

I sit on the steps and watch Ian leave. I should be with him.

Where is she?

Pretty soon Duncan and I are the only ones hanging around.

"Hey, shouldn't you be playing hockey with Ian?" Lilly asks, noticing me on the steps.

"My mom's not here."

"Oh, that's a drag." She sits down beside me. "Did you call her at work?"

"No, but that's a good idea. Will you stay with Duncan while I do that?"

"Sure."

I have to wait five minutes before a secretary notices me standing in the office.

"What's the matter, hon?" she asks. I tell her I need to call my mom, and she hands me the phone.

It takes a zillion rings before someone answers.

"King Thow Chinese Food."

"Can I speak to Annie, please?"

"She very busy right now. I take message?"

She's still at work!

My legs go tight. I'm so boiling mad right now, I can hardly speak.

Chapter Twelve

"So?" Lilly asks when I join her outside.

"She's still at work. I can't believe this! She promised."

"Maybe something happened, and she couldn't leave. That happens to my mom all the time," Lilly says.

"I want to go home!" Duncan says. He paces back and forth at the bottom of the stairs.

"I can still babysit if you want," Lilly offers.

"Really?"

"Sure."

"Hey, Duncan? Will you be okay if Lilly walks you home?"

"I like you, Mary Jane," Duncan says, grinning from ear to ear.

"I guess that's a yes." I smile at Lilly and then reach into my pocket for the key. "You'll need this for the back door. Duncan, you'll have to tell Mom who Lilly is."

"She's my girlfriend," Duncan giggles.

"He was talking about you at supper the other night. My mom thinks your name is Mary Jane for real."

"You were?" She smiles at Duncan. "How sweet is that? So, is there anything else I need to know?"

I'm in such a rush, I don't give her question much thought. "Nope," I say.

"Sounds like there's nothing to it then. Come on, Duncan. Let's go."

I fling my hockey gear to the ground, lace up my skates in record time and scan the pond for Cody. He's not here.

I check again.

Bonus, no Cody!

As I step onto the ice, the puck glides toward me. I bolt toward it like I'm Sidney Crosby. My stick scrapes against the ice as I maneuver the puck, not letting anyone at it.

"Go, Max!" Ian yells.

I dart in and out of the Red Eagles and make a shot. The puck hits one of the boots and bounces away from the net.

"Nice try," Ian says, skating toward me.

"That was just a practice shot, man. I'm just getting warmed up," I say as I race one of the Red Eagles up the pond.

It's like I'm playing for an Olympic gold medal and everything rides on this game. I snag the puck, break away and fake a pass before I move in for a shot on goal.

"And he scores!" Ian yells, raising his stick in the air.

I lean on my stick for a few seconds to catch my breath. The Red Eagles grab the puck and pass it a few times before Ian steals it and passes it to me. I dodge around them before I slam the puck into the net.

"And he scores again!" Ian hollers.

The whole game, I don't let up. In the end we win five to three.

"Way to play, Max!" Ian whacks my butt with his stick.

"I knew we needed you to win. Man, you can skate," Ian says.

"That was a blast." I sit down on the bench to remove my skates. "Boy, that was *sweet* Cody didn't show. I wonder where he was?"

"Haven't a clue," Ian says, taking off his skates.

"I wish I knew why he has such a hate-on for me. It's starting to really bug me."

"I know what ya mean." Ian rubs his foot. "Oh, man—my feet are numb. You ready to go?"

"Yup."

As we walk, I think about Cody until Ian says, "Man, I'm hungry!"

The words slam into my chest like one of his punches.

"Oh! No!"

"What's wrong?" Ian asks.

"I forgot to tell Lilly about Duncan's snack!"

"Lilly's not stupid. She'd get him something."

"But she won't know the only thing he eats after school is macaroni and cheese with a big blob of ketchup."

"You worry too much, Max," says Ian.

"Yeah, well, I have no choice."

When we reach my street, a fire truck is parked in front of my house with the red lights flashing. My legs go weak. I drop my gear and tear home, running as fast as I can.

"Wait up!" Ian yells.

Chapter Thirteen

The front door is wide open. Lilly is sitting on the sofa, crying.

"Oh, Max! I don't know what happened—"

"Where's Duncan?" I barely get the words out. A thick haze hangs in the air, and the smell of smoke burns my nose. My eyes start to water.

"Upstairs with Mr. Cooper," says Lilly.

I run past the firemen, taking the stairs two at a time. I hear Mr. Cooper's voice. "It's okay, Spider-Man…"

I stop at Duncan's door. He's huddled in the corner with his head tucked between his legs. He is rocking back and forth, making whimpering noises. Mr. Cooper is beside Duncan on his hands and knees, trying to calm him.

"Duncan?" I croak.

He lifts his head. He leaps up, runs full speed toward me and hugs me like he hasn't seen me in months. I squeeze back just as tight.

Duncan lets go of me, looks me right in the eyes and then hugs me again.

"What happened?" I ask.

Mr. Cooper stands up and starts explaining, but he is interrupted by a fireman calling up the stairs.

"Mr. Cooper? Are you planning on staying here until Mrs. O'Neil gets home?" the fireman asks.

"Yes, I'll be here," Mr. Cooper says.

"Okay, then, we're going to head out. Please have Mrs. O'Neil call the station."

"Thanks for your help," Mr. Cooper says.

I sit at the top of the stairs and lean against the railing. "What am I going to tell Mom? She's going to kill me."

"Let's just take it one minute at a time," Mr. Cooper says as he heads down the stairs. "I reckon the most important thing is that you're both all right."

I go check on Duncan. It looks like he's acting out a movie, although I don't recognize it. I lean against the door frame watching him pace around his room, shaking his hands rapidly and talking to himself.

"I'm hungry, Mouse. Where's Mary Jane? I want my macaroni and cheese. Mouse? Are you hungry too?" He pauses. "Mouse, I don't think Mary Jane is coming. Duncan has to think...Think. Think. Think. Just like Max does, just like Max. Oh no! Oh no!"

I can't take it any longer. I gently touch his shoulder. "Duncan, it's okay. Shhhhh, it's okay, buddy."

I pull him close. "You're safe. I'm sorry, Duncan. I'm really sorry."

"Max?" Ian whispers from the doorway.

"Be there in a second," I say.

I sit Duncan down on his bed and put his Spider-Man movie on. "I've got to go downstairs. I'll be back. I promise."

"I'll be back...I'll be back..." he repeats over and over.

"Is he going to be okay?" Ian asks as we head downstairs.

"I hope so."

I want to run away.

Lilly is buttoning up her coat by the front door. When she sees me, she starts crying again. "I'm so sorry, Max. When we got home, Duncan went straight upstairs to watch movies. I tried to hang out with him, but he didn't want me to." She sniffs. "He told me to go to the basement to watch TV. I wasn't downstairs for very long, I swear. And then I hear d him yelling. When I came upstairs, the stove was on fire…"

I can't speak. My eyes well up as I glance around the room. Everything in the kitchen is covered in a film of black soot. The cupboards above the stove are half burnt. White foam drips over the stove and onto the floor. The smell of smoke is stronger here, burning my eyes.

Mom—where are you?

Chapter Fourteen

"Oh my god!" Mom yells.

My body stiffens at the sound of her voice.

I automatically drop the cloth I'd been using to wipe down the walls. It lands in the bucket with a splash. Black soapy water splashes onto my pants.

"Oh no!" Mom drops the bags of Chinese food she was carrying when she enters the kitchen.

I can't move. My feet are stuck to the floor.

"Everyone's okay, Annie," Mr. Cooper steps in. "The boys had a little situation earlier."

"*What* happened?"

Before I can begin to explain, Duncan walks into the kitchen.

"I can't cook," he blurts out.

"You were cooking?"

"I don't like Mary Jane anymore," Duncan grumbles.

"Will someone tell me what's going on?"

I feel my cheeks burn up. "You never met us at school…" I say. "You promised."

"Joanne called in sick. I couldn't leave. Max, I left a message with one of the secretaries."

"I never got it," I say, looking at my feet.

"Well, I left one with…oh, what was her name?" She's getting worked up trying to remember it. Maybe she thinks I don't believe her.

"I think it was Lola. Yes! It was Lola!" She's talking really quickly now. "I brought supper home because I felt badly. I tried, Max…" Her voice cracks. "I really tried to get home. This is all my fault," she says. "I should have been here."

"Why don't we go talk somewhere private," Mr. Cooper suggests. He leads her into the living room.

"I guess she doesn't like the smell," Duncan says.

"Shhhh!" I stand in the hallway, where I can hear them.

"I'm having such a hard time on my own," she sobs. "I know Max has too many responsibilities, but I don't know what to do." She sniffs. "Dan would handle things so much better than me—"

"Now, Annie, don't sell yourself short," Mr. Cooper says. "Sometimes it's a matter of looking at things from a different angle." He pauses. "When my wife died, it took awhile for me to get my step back." He clears his throat. "But, Annie," he says gently, "your boys need you. I reckon asking for help isn't such a bad thing. "

I can't stand listening anymore. I head to my room.

"Max? Are you still awake?" Mom whispers from the doorway later that night. I don't answer. She comes in and sits on my bed. I keep perfectly still. "I'm so sorry, Max…" She sounds tired. I can tell she's been crying. "I know I need"—she takes a deep breath—

"some help. And I'm going to get it. Somehow." She sniffs. "I promise."

I hold my breath until she leaves. I'm wide awake now. My brain is whirling.

This is all my fault. I have to make things right, but how?

And then it hits me. I know what to do.

I slip downstairs once I hear her in the tub. I open the fridge and search for the cheese-slice package, but it's not there.

Then I remember throwing the wrapper out after making Duncan's sandwich. I root through the garbage and find it. I stare at the Kids Help Phone ad before taking it with me upstairs. My mind whirls as I pace around my room.

What do I say?

I rehearse a few lines in my head, but nothing sounds right. I crawl into bed with my phone and pull the covers over my head. Sometimes I think better in the dark. I lie there for a few minutes before

I reach under my bed for my flashlight. After pulling out some socks and hockey magazines, I find it.

I yank the blankets back over my head and shine the light on the number and dial. On the third ring, someone answers, "Kids Help Phone. How can I help you?"

I freeze.

"Hello? Anyone there?" the friendly voice asks. "It's okay if you're nervous. Take your time."

Panicked, I hang up.

I sit under the covers staring at the phone.

This is crazy.

I don't know what to tell them. They never show you that on their TV ads. I fiddle with the wrapper, thinking. Then I hear someone in the hallway. I turn off my flashlight and lay under the covers like I'm asleep.

In the middle of the night, I bolt awake. In my dream I had left Duncan alone, and he died. I tiptoe into his room. He's under the covers, snoring loudly. I peek into Mom's room. She's sound asleep too.

Relieved, I crawl back into bed. I'm now wide awake for the second time. The cheese wrapper crinkles in my bed. I decide I'm going to call. Taking a deep breath, I dial the number.

A friendly voice answers after the first ring.

"Kids Help Phone, Norene speaking. How can I help you?"

I bite my lip.

"Hello?"

"I'm here," I answer quietly.

"I thought I heard someone thinking on the other end of the line. What's up?"

Before I realize it, everything pours out of me. I tell her about the fire, Dad, Mom, Duncan.

Everything.

I even tell her about Cody. When I'm done, I feel a big weight lift off my shoulders.

"You've had quite a time, Max. I'm glad you called."

I sit up in my bed, hugging my knees as we talk. Everything she says makes sense—even the bit about Cody and how his meanness isn't about me or Duncan. It's about how he feels inside. And how change is hard, but that once you accept things it does get easier.

"Now, this information is for your mom. I think it might be helpful…"

I grab a pen and paper. I have to get it right.

"And, Max, if you need any more help, just call back. Someone will always be on the other end of this phone line, no matter what time it is."

I glance at the clock. It's 3:30 AM.

Chapter Fifteen

The sun streams into my room, making it hard to sleep. I yank the blankets over my head and lie there for a few minutes. I can hear Saturday-morning cartoons coming from Duncan's TV. He's got it turned up way too loud.

I glance at my clock. It's 8:00.

"Yes!" I whip off the blankets and jump out of bed. Mom's already in the shower when I knock on her door. Normally she'd be dead to the world. I guess she really did mean what she said last night.

I bang on the bathroom door. "Mom! Mom!"

"What's wrong?" she yells. "Is everything all right?"

"I've got tell you something! It's super important."

"Okay, okay…just give me a minute."

I plop down on her bed and wait.

"Okay, now what's so important?" she asks, coming out of the bathroom.

I begin to tell her, but I'm talking way too fast.

"Hey, hey, slow down," she says. "You called who?"

"The Kids Help Phone."

"Why would you call there?" She sits down beside me.

"Well, um, I wanted help. Here, I wrote it all down." I pass her the paper with all the information. "You're not going to believe it, Mom."

"What exactly did you tell this person?"

"A bunch of stuff."

"Like what, Max?"

I shrug my shoulders. "About the fire, and how everything has changed now that Dad's gone and…"

She stares at the note and then looks away.

"What's the matter, Mom? I thought you'd be happy."

"I can't believe you did this," she says, shaking her head.

I bite my lip. "I'm sorry, Mom. I was only trying to help." I glance down at my feet. It's not going right. Why isn't she happy? A lump lodges in my throat. "I'm really sorry about the kitchen and not staying with Duncan. I shouldn't have—"

She squeezes my hand. "The kitchen can be repaired, Max. I'm just thankful nothing more serious happened. I don't know what I'd do if I lost you boys." Her voice trails off. "You're all I have." She wipes her eyes. "You know, Mr. Cooper reminded me of something Daddy would have said."

"Like what?"

"Well, that we all make mistakes and do things we're not proud of. But if we learn from them, they're sort of a blessing."

She takes a deep breath. "Ever since Daddy died, I've been struggling to get through each day. I'm sorry things have been so tough for you." She pauses. "It's time I get back into the driver's seat. I've been in the backseat for far too long."

"I just want to play hockey," I say quietly. "It's the one thing that reminds me of Dad. It's weird, but when I skate, it's like he's right there with me."

Mom wraps her arms around me. "Let's take it one day at a time, and we'll see what we come up with." She kisses me on the top of my head and says, "Dad would be so proud of you."

"I miss him," I whisper.

"I do too."

We sit there for a few minutes not saying anything.

"You know, Max, you're just like him."

"I am?" I can feel myself grinning.

Mom smiles. "That you are."

"So, are you going to call?"

She looks at the note. "Of course I am. Why don't you let me get dressed and give me a minute to let this all sink in." She stares at the note. "I still can't believe you did this—for us."

Chapter Sixteen

The Family Hope Center is even better than the Kids Help Phone woman had described. Duncan has a bunch of new friends, but the best thing is, he gets his own support worker. She'll be with him after school until Mom gets home.

"It's taking a long time," Duncan says while we're waiting for the worker to arrive for the first time.

"Hey, I think she's here!" I yell.

Duncan stops pacing and joins me in front of the window.

Mom turns off the kettle and slips in between us. We stand together like sardines stuffed in a tin can, watching her get out of a little yellow Volkswagen.

"I like her," Duncan says.

"Her name is Alison," Mom says.

"My Lady Alison," Duncan corrects her.

Mom and I laugh.

"So where are we going?" I ask Mom later on that night.

"You'll see," she says, pulling out of the driveway and heading up the hill toward the school. I have no clue what she's up to. She parks at the entrance to the path into the woods and turns off the car.

"It's dark out," Duncan announces.

"There's actually a full moon," Mom says. Then she looks at me.

"Are we really doing what I think we're doing?" I ask.

"Last one on the pond is a rotten egg."

"For real?"

She nods.

"But, you—"

"I don't like rotten eggs," Duncan butts in.

"Don't worry," Mom says, turning to face Duncan. "I brought you hot chocolate."

"Good," he says in his deep voice.

Everything glows in the moonlight. The sky looks lit up. The trees rustle slightly in the breeze. Our boots crunch over the crisp snow. Even Duncan seems caught up in the magic of the night. He doesn't say a word. I still can't believe we're doing this with Mom.

"Oh my goodness, it's beautiful," she says, breaking the silence. "No wonder you and Dad came here at night."

"I like hot chocolate," Duncan says.

"You're always moving us along, aren't you, Duncan." Mom sits on the bench next to me while I tie up my skates. She pulls out the thermos and pours Duncan a cup of hot chocolate.

"I wish Dad was here," I say quietly. "It doesn't feel right being here at night without him."

Mom puts her arm around me and rests her head on my shoulder. We sit there not saying anything. Shadows dance on the ice when clouds pass over the moon. In a quiet voice, she finally says, "Can I fill in for him?"

"But you don't have skates."

"I can use these." She pulls out a pair of black skates.

Dad's skates. I feel a pang in my chest.

"I know I have big skates to fill," she says. "But with a couple of pairs of hockey socks and a little help from you and Duncan, hopefully I won't break my neck." She squeezes my hand. "And when you're bigger, you can have them."

I'm glad it's dark so Mom can't see my tears. "Thanks," I croak. "I'd like that."

It isn't until I step onto the ice that I notice real hockey nets on the pond. "Hey, look at the nets!" I squeal. "I wonder where they came from?" I turn toward Mom.

She grins from ear to ear. "Me," she says quietly.

"They're great! Wait until Ian sees them!" I whack the puck toward the net but miss.

"I'll get it," Duncan says, leaping up from the bench, spilling hot chocolate everywhere.

"I might need a hand," Mom says, hobbling toward the edge of the pond.

She looks like a little kid learning how to walk as she tries to skate. Dad's skates are way too big for her. I skate over to help her. "I think you might need to get your own pair, Mom."

"I think you're right. I can hardly stand up in these things."

Mom holds on to me tightly. We both start to laugh.

"Mom!" Duncan yells.

"What?" she says and then giggles as she tries to take another glide.

"You're laughing."

Author Notes

Asking for help is a sign of true strength.

In Canada, Kids Help Phone is a free professional service for anyone aged twenty years and younger. You can call anytime of day or night, 365 days a year, about anything, from trouble with your homework to dealing with the loss of a loved one, from feelings of depression to thoughts of suicide. You don't have to tell them who you are, and your information is safe. In other words, your call is anonymous and confidential. The number is 1-800-668-6868.

If talking to someone is a bit intimidating right now, you could log on to the Kids Help Phone website and get help from professional counselors, online. Reading what other kids are talking about can also make you feel less alone. Check it out. It's pretty neat. All you need to do is type in the words Kids Help Phone or www.kidshelpphone.ca.

If you live in the United States, there are similar services, such as Boys Town (1-800-448-3000, www.boystown.org) or Nineline (1-800-999-9999, www.nine-line.org). You can also talk to a teacher or guidance counselor at your school.

Many years ago, I volunteered on the Adult Help Phone in Nova Scotia. I'm very thankful to my friend Nancy Allen, who encouraged me to do it with her. Being a friendly voice on the other end of the phone was a very rewarding experience. Someone—somewhere— is waiting to be that friendly voice for you.

Acknowledgments

I have many people to thank.

Deep gratitude goes to my writing group: Jo Ann Yhard, Lisa Harrington, Graham Bullock, Jennifer Thorne and Joanna Butler. The friendship, insight and trust we share is more than I could hope for—truly a writer's dream. A big thank-you also goes to Norene Smiley for putting us all together and setting us on our writing paths.

I'm very grateful to Melanie Jeffs for her keen editorial eye and for guiding me in such a way that allowed my creative juices to unfold to make the story richer. I will be forever grateful to Orca Book Publishers for believing in my story.

To Donna Hansplant (former Vice-President of the Kids Help Phone) for taking the time to read my manuscript and for giving it a thumbs-up!

Thanks to Cynthia d'Entremont, who effortlessly comes up with smashing book titles. *Maxed Out* suits this story perfectly.

To my dear friends, who have cheered me along the way.

To my parents, who taught me to find the good in every situation. This helped me immensely when trying to find something positive from rejection letters—which I did. Each one pushed me to get things right.

To my cousin Alison for her sense of fun, seeing love in all things and for bringing Michael into the world.

And finally to my husband Ken, my rock—who has always believed in me. To my children, Emma, Maude, Rose and Grace—may you always believe in yourselves and know that the sky is the limit if you follow your dreams.